THE GREEK MUSEUMS

Benaki Museum

Translation: Kay Cicellis

THE GREEK MUSEUMS

Benaki Museum

MANOLIS CHATZIDAKIS

Director of the Byzantine Museum

EKDOTIKE ATHENON S.A.

Athens 1978

Erste Verlag 1975
Zweite Verlag 1976
Dritte Verlag 1977
Vierte Verlag 1978

Druck und Einband durch
EKDOTIKE HELLADOS S.A.
Eine Schwestergesellschaft
der EKDOTIKE ATHENON S.A.
8. Philadelphiasstr., Athen

FROM ANCIENT TO POPULAR GREEK ART

THE BENAKI MUSEUM: The Building

In the heart of Athens, across the street from the National Park, stands one of the few great residences that have survived in that section of Vasilissis Sophias Avenue. These elegant houses were built around 1900 for upper-class families of Athens in a pleasing traditional style. The neoclassical building across the Park, with its portico of Doric columns and marble balconies and jambs, was bought and enlarged by Emmanuel Benaki, a national benefactor from Alexandria, when he decided to settle in Athens. The house was the work of the architect Anastasios Metaxas. After completing the necessary alterations and additions, Emmanuel's son Anthony Benaki, used it in 1930 to house his personal art collections and to establish in it the Benaki Museum.

The Benaki collections and the founding of the Museum

Anthony Benaki (1873-1954) was an important cotton merchant in Egypt, and his wealth enabled him to acquire a considerable number of works of art. In 1927, upon settling in Athens, he devoted himself to a number of civic projects but mainly to the organization of this museum. When this young patrician, lover of art and sport, began buying precious Oriental weapons, he probably did not have in mind to found a fully-equipped museum. But thirty years spent in the methodical selection and purchase of works of art from Egypt, Greece, and the world market in Western Europe resulted in the accumulation of a vast number of valuable objects, which eventually came to form almost complete series of important works of art in diverse fields. With the contentment of a mature collector and the ambition to render an important public service, Anthony Benaki decided in 1927 to found a museum — a μουσεῖον in the best cultural sense of this ancient term — and to offer it to the Nation.

Anthony Benaki's personal contribution

His donation was not limited to the signing of a formal contract with the State, but included his own services as well — the personal labour of a highly experienced collector of cultivated taste who also possessed the will and the power to substantiate the dream begotten by his enthousiastic imagination.

It took him three years of incessant work to extend and convert his father's house into a museum. Emmanuel Benaki's other heirs all gladly offered their share of the inheritance for this purpose. It was also necessary to design hundreds of show-cases, frames, and stands and to study the problems of lighting and of the protection of the exhibits from exposure. The most perfect devices known at the time were used throughout. Every single item, from the extension and conversion of the building down to the last detail, was decided by him personally.

Owing to the great diversity of the collections, the disposition of the rooms in the museum presented difficulties, and there were also practical problems arising from the transformation of a building designed for family life into a museum. This task required not only sound knowledge and a fine sense of the materials involved and of the chromatic and tactile quality of each exhibit, but also considerable inventiveness in finding practical solutions. Anthony Benaki combined these qualities to an astonishing degree. He set up his museum almost single-handed. Thousands of objects, whether works of fine art or pieces of native handicraft, all chosen through a lifetime of judicious collecting, were arranged by him and exhibited in 270 show-cases and on the walls of 24 rooms. This purely personal offering was perhaps even more valuable than the huge amounts of money spent on purchasing the collections and on installing and endowing the museum.

Benaki did not consider his mission completed with the foundation and endowment of the museum. After its inauguration and incorporation as an autonomous foundation in 1931, he continued to enrich it with admirable new acquisitions; he also supervised and financed the training of specialized personnel, the compilation of catalogues by Greek and foreign scholars of world repute, and the publication of a large two-volume album containing coloured illustrations of Greek national costumes. Until 1942, all these expenses were met by Benaki himself; it was only during the dark years of the enemy occupation of Greece that he was compelled to ask the Government to grant the museum some financial assistance, mainly in order to enable the staff of the Museum to survive in those difficult times. This assistance has continued since then in the form of a State subsidy.

When World War II was declared in 1939, Benaki began to pack the museum exhibits in special cases with his own hands, working many hours every day for several months. It was with the same untiring devotion that he set up the museum once again after the liberation of Greece, adding new show-cases and planning additional improvements.

A perfect identification of the creator with his creation, touchingly expressed in Benaki's testament by the wish to have his heart walled in the museum, was the essential factor that bound together diverse collections in a unified whole. This personal touch, guided as it was by good taste rather than by any rigid prescriptions for chronological or geographical classification, is nevertheless impressively convincing, generating an atmosphere of warm intimacy in a museum whose rooms have retained the aspect of a private residence. The arrangement of the exhibits has also retained the character of a personal collection, and this is what distinguishes the Benaki Museum from museums of a strictly specialized nature.

The spirit of an age

At about this time, Greek intellectuals were turning their attention to the art of medieval and modern Greece. It is no coincidence that the first Byzantine museum in Greece was founded at about this time, or that Photis Kontoglou, a painter and writer working in the Byzantine manner, emerged on the scene with a school of followers. There was also a marked trend toward folk art, which soon became the object of intensive study and at times even of emulation. The work of Angelike Chatzimichali, A. Zachos, and others in this field, the Delphic festivals organized by Angelos and Eve Sikelianos, and the multitude of societies and exhibitions devoted to these new concerns were also parts of this trend. Anthony Benaki enthusiastically helped all these manifestations with financial contributions and his personal prestige. Yet it was his museum that gave the movement a permanently tangible expression. Thus seen, it stands as testimony to the intellectual and aesthetic aspirations of a generation in an era which may have been fraught with difficulties but which was also culturally flourishing.

The donors

The high educational mission with which Benaki wished to invest his museum from its very inception and the scrupulous care taken in the presentation, annotation, and preservation of the exhibits quickly raised the Benaki Museum to a position of great prestige. From the very beginning, various organizations and individuals entrusted the museum with the valuable relics and works of art in their possession. The Exchange of Populations Foundation donated some of the religious treasures which had been brought to Greece by refugees from Asia Minor, the Pontos, and Eastern Thrace in 1923; the Eleutherios Venizelos Foundation presented it with that great statesman's files and a series of memorabilia which had belonged to him; more recently, the St. Dekozis - Vouros Foundation offered to finance the construction of a two-story wing to house lecture halls and exhibition rooms.

As regards individual donors, G. Eumorphopoulos gave the museum his collection of Chinese pottery, complete with appropriate show-cases. Damianos Kyriazis donated his large collections of embroideries; pottery; drawings, water-colours and lithographs on Greek themes; a considerable number of rare books; and massive historical records. The room that bears his name was built also at his own expense. After several sporadic donations, Mrs. Helen Antoniou Stathatos offered the wood-carved panelling of a drawing-room from an 18th century upper-class residence in Kozani. This donation was accompanied by icons, embroideries, lithographs, jewellery, and miscellaneous other items. Through a State grant a special room was added to shelter the panelling and her other donations. Other donors were Marina Lappa-Diomedous, Christian Lampikis, and Mr. Loukas Benakis, to mention only some of the major donors. With the exception of the Chinese pottery collection donated by Eumorphopoulos, all these donations came to complete the original collections of Anthony Benaki. This role of the museum as a repository in which private collections of varying sizes, and personal records of special interest may be preserved for posterity is yet another, no less important, function of the Benaki Museum.

THE EXHIBITS

To grasp the underlying unity that pervades the various collections, it might be useful to think of the exhibits as belonging to a pattern of three intersecting circles. The first circle consists of Greek works of art, from prehistoric times to the modern age. The emphasis here is on ancient Greek goldsmith's work and Byzantine and post-Byzantine art, including painting and miniature work. The second circle, which overlaps with the first, is devoted to modern Greek themes. These exhibits occupy most of the rooms of the museum. They represent Greek folk art in all its aspects together with similar specimens from the folk art of other countries; modern Greek historical relics; an important section of the Historical Archives; a large collection of drawings, water-colours, and lithographs picturing landscapes, scenes from everyday life, and various characters of modern Greece — all of them by foreign artists of the Romantic period; and also important informative material, whether in the form of documents or of art works related to Western philhellenism. The third circle consists of collections of minor arts and handicraft from the Eastern Mediterranean, both the coastal areas and the hinterland. This circle overlaps with both the preceding ones; for instance, the large collection of weapons includes Islamic and European masterpieces as well as Greek historical relics.

These three closely interdependant circles and the manner in which the collections are exhibited offer an eloquent picture of the unity of Greek tradition through the ages, not only in Greece proper, but across the whole area which received the impact of Hellenism in the course of centuries. In the field of folk art they also point to the existence of an essential affinity between neighbouring civilizations. Here are a few examples: the gold objects, which make up a separate collection, show a surprising continuity in certain techniques from the Mycenaean age to our own day. The Fayyum portraits of Greek art from Egypt (3rd and 4th centuries A.D.) refer us directly to the sources of Byzantine hagiographic portraiture. Works of religious minor art in metal, bone, wood, or gold reveal an unbroken continuity of this exquisite and costly type of craftsmanship from the early Byzantine years to the liberation of Greece in 1821. Here again, post-Byzantine minor art forms the connecting link between Byzantine art and the folk art of modern Greece. Classicizing Egyptian fabrics from the 4th to the 7th centuries A.D., of which there are many beautiful specimens in the museum, are clearly seen to lead to the museum's fine collection of Muslim fabrics of a later date, one of the largest in the world. To the discerning spectator, the relation between these fabrics and more recent Greek handwoven materials is quite evident. Finally, Byzantine ceramics, hardly distinguishable in some cases from contemporaneous Muslim ones, find their natural continuation in the ceramic works of modern Greek folk art. It is obvious that the projection of Greek art, in all its ramifications, contacts, and influences throughout the centuries, had been the collector's unwavering air.

Gold jewellery: ancient

This collection is one of the most interesting in the Benaki Museum. It includes some quite unique specimens as, for instance, the two gold cups of the third millennium B.C., which have apparently come from Northern Euboia (fig. 2). Their clearcut shapes have their counterparts in silver and ceramic ware, and so has their decoration of impressed parallel lines. Recent research in this field ascribe these cups to the transitional period between the Neolithic and the Bronze ages in Greece — the period known as Chalcolithic (3,000 B.C.). The funerary band from Kos, decorated with miniature sphinxes and rosettes, densely clustered together, is a rare example of the goldsmith's skill, worthy of Daedalic art (fig. 5a). The technique is still intensely Orientalizing, as in the jewels from Kameiros in Rhodes dating from the same period.

The fine Late Hellenistic specimens in the museum originally belonged to the so-called "Thessalian treasure", the larger part of which was donated by Mrs. H.A. Stathatos to the National Archaeological Museum. The jewellery with its variety of techniques in filigree, granulation, and enamel, and the way in which motifs are selected and arranged, betrays a long tradition of technical skill and wisdom, and must be ascribed to the region of Macedonia. The goldsmiths living in the vicinity of Mount Pangaion where there were gold mines, were renowned for their skill throughout the centuries. The great diadem (fig. 5b) is one of the most opulent specimens both as regards the materials used and the variety of techniques involved; it is also one of the most elegant pieces of jewellery of its kind. The necklace with three rows of miniature amphorae testifies to the same high craftsmanship, albeit with a tendency to excessive elaboration, as regards the number and rows of pendants, which is typical of the 3rd century B.C. (fig. 6b). The "knot of Herakles" too was fashionable mainly during the 3rd century B.C.

Because most of the antique jewels that have come down to us were found in tombs, their subjects always have some religious significance, even when their obvious purpose is the achievement of elegance and the display of skill. On a charming earringS (fig. 6a), a Muse is playing the lyre in the midst of luxuriant vegetation. On the head of a pin, of a kneeling Aphrodite — a theme common in Hellenistic art — on top of a capital is surrounded by four small Cupids (fig. 3). On a pair of earrings, hanging Cupids — those small winged infants of no particular significance — are shown wearing the garments of an Oriental god, who is a sort of a combination of Adonis and Attis (fig. 4).

Gold jewellery: Byzantine

Byzantine goldsmiths carried on the Roman technique of polychrome stones and gold leaf rather than solid gold, and also developed the enamel technique. With the help of small gold plates which outlined the design and encased the coloured enamel, it became possible to produce complete, detailed representations. This technique is known as "gold cloisonné enamel" (fig. 7d). A fairly large number of 6th and 7th century jewels, which have reached us as part of the caches or "treasures" that had been hidden away by their owners to safeguard them from invasions and raids, shows that pagan elements progressively disappear, giving way to Christian symbols, such as crosses, ivy leaves, peacocks, and monograms until the main Byzantine era, when the dominant figures are finally those of Christ and various Christian saints (figs. 7d and 9).

Gold jewellery: post-Byzantine

Religious worship demanded a certain opulence in the materials used for liturgical books and sacred vessels in order to enhance their importance. Besides, the principal objects used during the Liturgy, such as the Gospel, the chalice, the incense-burners, the incense-boats, the cloth used for covering the chalice, and all the other ceremonial articles, are displayed to the congregation during the offertory procession and must therefore present an imposing appearance. This is the reason why even during Turkish rule, when money was scarce, craftsmen working in metal — mainly silver — continued to enrich the enamel used with precious stones. The same costly techniques were used for secular articles intended for the Christian and non-Christian nobility, and to this end flourishing handicraft industries existed in certain large cities. It is known that there were many fine Greek goldsmiths in Constantinople, whose work must have been of the same high quality as that of the buckle with the many inlaid stones in the elegant Persian style (fig. 8). A similar technique was used for the jewellery which was made in Constantinople in 1692 for the mother of Peter the Great of Russia and which in inventories of that period is described as "Greek handiwork". Enamel was not much used in works of this kind; as painted enamel, it was used much more extensively for the decoration of the one side of episcopal pendants, their other side being usually decorated with precious stones, such as sapphires, emeralds and diamonds, set in the characteristic style of Constantinople. A good example is the pendant of Bishop Parthenios of Caesarea, dating from 1738 (fig. 11). The same workshops are probably responsible for Parthenios' crosier, decorated with enamel and stones, and made in the same year (fig. 29).

Enamel was put to a different use on the Greek islands, where jewellery was usually made in the form of graceful ships. In marriage-contracts dating from that time, these miniature ships are referred to as "Venetika" (Venetians), which seems to point to the possibility that they may have been made in Venice by Greek goldsmiths in the 17th and 18th centuries. There is sufficient evidence supporting this possibility, for many ornaments and jewels did come from Venice during that period, and there were many Greek goldsmiths living in Venice at that time. The earrings with three-mast caravels in the museum confirm this assumption: one side of the ship's flag pictures the Lion of St. Mark, while the other bears the name of the donor: IΩ(άννης) ΜΠ(άος) (fig. 48). Larger enamel ships in the form of pendants, in a similar style and of the same origin, are to be found among the votive offerings in the monastery of Patmos (fig. 1).

Silverware

To return to religious ornaments, among the oldest and finest post-Byzantine works is an incense-boat of 1613 from Macedonia (fig. 27) which carries on the Byzantine tradition of using architectural forms in minor arts. In skylights, this tradition skillfully combines gold-plated silver with polychrome enamel. A similar tendency to incorporate various less distinct architectural forms may be attributed to the infuence of some incense-burners from the Northern Balkans mostly from Rumania and Transylvania, which imitate Gothic turret-shaped buildings, as in the incense-burner with a handle (fig. 28).

The covers of liturgical books are usually made of silver with embossed representations referring to the contents of the particular book (fig. 21). The degree of skill displayed in these book-covers depends very much on the region in which they were made and on how prosperous the region happened to be. Workshops in Asia Minor usually produced less refined specimens, whereas those in Western Greece betray Italian influence; in Moldovlachia, on the other hand, the over-elaborate ornamentation is often due to the influence of folk art.

Later silverwork preserved forms and types of liturgical articles which were in use in the early Church. The Orthodox liturgy, which has remained practically unchanged through the ages, and the unbroken technical and artistic traditions of Orthodoxy have kept these forms alive in all their fundamental elements, although they each bear the distinctive marks of their time and place of origin. Thus the metal flabella which participate in litanies and precede the offertory procession in the Great Entry during the liturgy have kept the form, even to the perforated ornamentation and decorative motifs, of their early prototypes. The finely-worked circular flabella of 1690 (fig. 31), in addition to the usual conventional features, also includes a perforated centerpiece incised in the Persian style of the 17th century, while the technique of using gold-plated embossed motifs on a flat silver background is at least as old as classicizing Byzantine silverwork of the 6th and 7th centuries. Even the silver cross shown on fig. 32, dating as late as the 19th century, represents a continuation of the ancient tradition of large silver or bronze crosses intended for processional litanies, though it is adapted in form to the large wooden cross which usually crowns the iconostasis in post-Byzantine churches.

Sacerdotal vestments also betray a survival of old forms, not necessarily stemming from religious tradition. The bishop's mitre, though it came into general use only as late as the 16th century, retains the shape and decoration of the imperial head-dresses of the Byzantine age. A rather rare silver mitre in the museum (fig. 30) is a good example: under a series of arches, there are embossed gold-plated representations, with incised details, of the Deesis and various scenes from the Gospels. This mitre comes from the community of Argyroupolis in the Pontos, and the workmanship has that same rough quality as we find in silverware of the same period (17th century) in Georgia and the Caucasus.

Christian Egypt

The Early Christian collections from Egypt, especially of textiles and bone objects, are among the finest and largest, although there are also impressive collections of objects in bronze, wood, pottery, and other materials. Only a few pieces are shown in this volume, but they are sufficient to indicate a strong classical tradition in the Graeco-Roman and Hellenized cities of Egypt. Roman rule, which succeeded the Greeks in Egypt, encouraged the admixture of heterogeneous elements. This was an inevitable consequence of the long years of contact between the ruling Graeco-Roman world and the local religious and artistic traditions that still lived on among the upper classes of the Egyptian people. There was also some contact with African elements in the regions of the Sudan and Aswan. At times, this relationship lent a particular tone to artistic manifestations in Egypt in the early centuries of the Christian era, although on the whole, these manifestations never did move very far from the common artistic language prevailing at the time across the whole eastern basin of the Mediterranean. The funerary portraits found in considerable numbers, particularly in the Fayyum area, are typical examples. They reflect beliefs specifically related to Egyptian religion: the immortal soul, the "kâ", upon returning to the mummified body, must be able to recognize it without difficulty. But the techniques used in these innumerable portraits are the same as those used in cities as far apart as Pompei and Palmyra; in other words, these techniques followed a pattern of traditions which had influenced each other in the course of their evolution within that extensive area of the world. In the better examples, the effort is to render the human face realistically and to depict the psychological make-up and racial traits of the deceased individual. As a result, these portraits present a picture of Middle-Eastern humanity which corresponds quite closely to that of today.

The two portraits in encaustic wax technique represent two different trends. The male portrait (fig. 12) depicts with striking simplicity a complete human being: with a bit of brilliantly white cloth next to the purple face against a grey background. The face seems to project out of its narrow frame; the modelling is emphatic, and the eyes seem to gaze as if lost in memories. The hair-arrangement and various other features place it in the mid-3rd century A.D. In the second portrait, belonging to the 4th or 5th century A.D. (fig. 13), the modelling of the woman's face is more linear and the expression more extrovert; the subject was perhaps depicted full-size, which explains why her priestly gestures acquire a special significance. The hieratic Egyptian cross — the "ankh" — in her left hand may indicate that she was a Christian, for this type of cross had a double significance.

The impact of paintings in the Greek style upon decorative crafts, particularly heavy woollen handwoven materials used as wall-hangings or curtains, is shown in a piece of material representing a youthful figure in contours only; the great eyes retain, even as late as the 5th or 6th century A.D., vestiges from the painted portraits of Fayyum. The figure may have been meant to personify one of the four seasons (fig. 14).

The great thematic repertory of Egyptian textiles, that have survived in large numbers thanks to the dry soil in which they were found often includes themes from Sassanid Persia as, for instance, the finely drawn and brilliantly coloured winged Pegasus of the 5th or 6th century A.D. (fig. 15).

Among the most characteristic products of Egyptian minor arts of Christian era, often erroneously referred to as "Coptic", are objects of carved bone. The figures which decorate these bone objects, often only in a fragmentary manner, are survivals of Greek mythology: Nereids, Silenoi, Dionysoi, etc. The Benaki Museum collection, enriched by the Loukas Benakis donation, is one of the finest of its kind; but, here, a comb is singled out from the initial collection; it is carved on both sides and probably served some official function (fig. 17 top, right). The representation on each side is the personification of a city — probably Constantinople and Alexandria — in the form of an enthroned queen wearing the typical crown made of city ramparts known as a "polos". In these rather schematic seated figures, devoid of elegance, yet emanating a certain majesty, one can discern the transformation which the robust and imposing figures of Rome underwent in the course of time.

This should not be taken as a clumsy imitation of a classical prototype, but as the expression of a new aesthetic ideal, which was to characterize the art of the Middle Ages.

Small Byzantine sculptures

On the small carved plaques which were made in Constantinople during the reign of the Macedonian dynasty in the 9th and 10th centuries, the classicizing tastes of the aristocracy expressed themselves over a fairly considerable length of time in a revival of subjects and techniques from the Hellenistic and Roman traditions. The martial Saint George on an ivory plaque (fig. 17 left) is but an anaemic echo of this trend.

The small relief plaques of steatite —a soft, non-porous stone with soapy surfaces— are much more Byzantine in character. Since steatite was a much cheaper material than ivory, it became widely used during less prosperous periods, such as the 12th and 13th centuries. This stone, coming in shades of greenish grey, was covered with gold and various colours, a technique also applied to carved marble iconostases. The plaque picturing the Annunciation (fig. 17 bottom, right) retains easily visible traces of gold, red, and black paint, which seems to explain why the carving was rather carelessly done. The plaque depicting the Presentation at the Temple (fig. 18) is much more elaborate. The symmetrical composition is conventional enough, but the distinctive feature here is the triangular arrangement, emphasized by the tall arched baldachin and the slender, elegant figures, reminiscent of those produced during the late Komnenian period. The carved draperies, however, serene and rhythmical, hark back to classicizing prototypes.

Miniature painting

The two miniature paintings that decorate either side of a sheet of parchment (figs. 19-20), once belonging to a Mount Athos codex now at Dumbarton Oaks, also belong to the classicizing tradition. The codex, written and painted in 1084, contains the Psalter and the New Testament, illustrated with numerous miniature paintings taking up most of each page. It belongs to a type of Psalter known as "aristocratic", because the richness and skill of the miniature paintings and illuminated capitals, as well as the written text itself, reflect various trends of this fine art in Constantinople during the second half of the 11th century. The fine, almost weightless figures, the near-transparent draperies, the landscape with highlighted cliff-tops, are the main distinctive features in both works. Yet, in one of these, Jonah emerges from the whale, accompanied by a personification of the Deep, and the subtle gradation of colour in the landscape suggests a sense of atmospheric perspective, whereas in the second painting, picturing the Three Children in the Fiery Furnace, the composition unfolds on two parallel levels. Although both these works are by the same painter, they seem to follow different prototypes.

Icons

The revival of this classicizing tradition can best be observed in the portable icons of the Palaiologan dynasty. One that is among the better-known icons of that period represents the Hospitality of Abraham; it must have decorated the entrance to the Prothesis in the iconostasis, which explains its elongated, rectangular shape (fig. 23). The composition, a symbolic representation of the Holy Trinity, this supreme Christian doctrine, is perfectly adapted to this shape. The peaceful scene, with its gentle, ethereal, angelic figures and abstracted faces, represents a peak in the idealistic movement at the end of the 14th century. Space becomes meaningless; one can only just tell apart the plane of the angels from that of the buildings; the emphasis is on the decorative elements: the vertical and horizontal features of the conventional architectural forms enclose as in a frame the ellipsoid group of figures, and the dabs of colour dance about with a pleasing rhythm as if across a sparkling surface.

The 15th century triptych, representing themes from Mount Athos, such as the miraculous Virgin Portaëtissa from the Iviron Monastery, Saint Paul of the Xeropotamos Monastery, and Saint Eleutherios (fig. 22), continues a trend of the Palaiologian style of painting which was in direct contrast to the classicizing tradition mentioned above. In this kind of works, there is a concern in giving more life to the face, without avoiding either grimacing or ugliness; this is well in keeping with the emphatic modelling and the broad, highlighted surfaces in the paintings. We have here a continuation of the anti-classical trend which can also be seen in several other works, as in the 14th century large icon of Christ from Thessalonike in the Byzantine Museum.

The tall, slender, airy figure of Saint Demetrios, with its rather sickly, expressionless, and faintly-lit face and the spindly legs, is the work of a Cretan painter of about 1500 (fig. 24). During this period, when the post-Byzantine Cretan school of painting first began to take shape, the themes and techniques appeared as a continuation of the Late Palaiologan period, quite frequently without any trace of Italian influences. However, Cretan painters were also capable of painting in the Italian style. An example of this kind of painting is the Adoration of the Magi, signed Domenikos (fig. 25). There is no reason why this painting in the Venetian manner, reminiscent of Bassano, should not be the work of the famous Cretan painter Domenico Theotocopuli, otherwise known as El Greco, painted when he was still a simple hagiographer in Crete in 1565 or thereabouts. His later apprenticeship under the great Venetian masters brought out the latent artistic potentialities which finally led him to produce works ranking among the highest in European painting.

Cretan painting, profoundly religious in content, reached its peak during the 17th century, producing a number of well-known artists. The Benaki collection of Cretan paintings includes outstanding works by both well-known and anonymous painters of the Cretan school. The icon shown on fig. 26 is the work of Theodore Poulakis, one of the most industrious Cretan painters, who divided his time between Venice and Corfu. When he wished to be up-to-date, he used as his models copper-plate engravings by the Flemish engraver Sadeler, and when he wished to be conservative, he used as models the better-known Cretan painters of the 16th century with a marked preference for George Klotzas. In this large complex icon entitled Hymn to the Virgin Mary, he was certainly inspired by a well-known icon by George Klotzas which was quite original for its time and which presented a certain narrative loquacity in its details. But, in the bottom part of the composition, Poulakis enriched his subject with additional scenes from the Second Coming, and, here, his rather baroque temperament betrays a fondness for dramatic scenes which are hardly at all Byzantine.

Asia Minor ceramics

This relatively small collection includes some of the finest products of this art from Asia Minor; the so-called Rhodian pottery, although it comes from Nicaea and Kütahya, both cities in Asia Minor, where it flourished between the 16th and 18th centuries. Here are a few typical specimens made for the Greek islands, where multicoloured ceramics were in great demand and, together with embroideries, formed the main ornaments of island homes: a plate picturing a three-mast ship with all its sails unfurled (fig. 33); an elegantly-shaped flask picturing fast-sailing boats (fig. 38); and a small jug picturing young he-goats arranged heraldically (fig. 37). All of these must certainly reflect Greek artistic tastes. The plate with the picture of a lion and a Greek religious inscription of 1666 (fig. 34) belongs to a different category. Dishes of this kind were made to be inserted into the outer walls of churches as a decorative feature. The egg-shaped objects (fig. 35-36) were also intended for churches; they were hung from chandeliers, having replaced the more common ostrich eggs. These eggs, as well as other ceramic objects for church use, of no great value, were still being made in Kütahya in the 18th century.

Embroideries. Local costumes

These ceramic plates introduced into the Greek home a taste of the Orient, featuring smooth flat colouring and Persian floral patterns.

The embroideries now to be discussed are the result of this acquaintance with Oriental decorative styles although they are the work of Greek women living in the islands or elsewhere in Greece. The

Benaki collection of embroideries is extremely rich and contains specimens from every part of Greece; there is an enormous variety as regards geographical distribution, local tradition, and contact with other lands.

In the Skyros embroideries, the more common motifs are ships, flowers, imaginary woodcocks, young warriors brandishing swords, on foot or on horseback, and other enchanting subjects (figs. 40,43,44). All these have their own native quality, in both the strictly local and the wider Greek sense, regardless of their original ancestry. The Skyros embroideries differ considerably from those of other islands as, for instance, those of Crete, which may be polychrome or monochrome, but almost invariably contain certain steadily recurring motifs, like Gorgons and two-headed eagles amidst dense vegetation with clearly Western reverberations (figs. 41, 45). In contrast, the Jannina embroideries show a preference for Oriental floral patterns inspired from textiles, which makes them more akin to the Skyros specimens. In the wedding processions embroidered on nuptial pillow-cases, which feature richly attired horsemen, bridegrooms, brides, and attendants, the costumes are ostentatiously opulent; the prototypes in this case are to be found in the West or in Moldovlachia (fig. 42).

There is also great variety in the national costumes of Greece, whether those worn on special occasions or those intended for daily use; each region, not to say each village, had its own costume. The Benaki Museum collection, not all of which is on show, is the most complete and important of its kind, and thus affords a good opportunity for a thorough study of the subject of Greek folk costume in all its variety. We shall only note here the unerring taste and high technical skill in the execution of the costumes as regards both the main lines, the tailoring, cutting, and sewing of each part, and the embroidered ornamentation in gold or coloured threads. These skills would indicate that the making of costumes was a professional occupation. Jannina was a famous centre of costume manufacturing, covering even export requirements for remote regions (fig. 46).

Wood-carving

During the centuries of Turkish rule, wood-carving retained a consistently high quality, because painted and gilt wooden iconostases and other church furnishings made of wood, had replaced the marble screen of earlier periods. During the 18th century, Western Macedonia became an important wood-carving centre, serving Northern Greece and the neighbouring Balkan countries. Perhaps as a result of Western influence, it was the custom for the wealthier houses in that region to have rooms covered with finely carved wood-panelling. A reception-room of this kind from a residence in Kozani has been offered the Museum by Mrs. H.A. Stathatos (fig. 50). During that period, a certain degree of prosperity resulting from trade relations with Western Europe led to the construction of handsome large houses in the cities of Macedonia, combining in their decoration western styles with Oriental or purely local motifs. The skilled wood-carvers of Macedonia knew how to harmonize the flourishing local tradition with the cultured tastes of travelled Greeks. In this way the arts underwent a continuous process of renewal under the foreign rule that dominated the Hellenic world.

1. *Pendant from Patmos, in the shape of a caravel, with gold,*
enamel, and pearls. Probably Venetian, 18th century.

1

2. One of a pair of gold cups decorated with systems of lines. Found in Northern Euboia and probably dated to the Chalcolithic period (3000 B.C.), these cups are unique as specimens of craftsmanship in gold in that remote period between the Neolithic and the Bronze ages in Greece.

3. Head of a pin in the shape of a capital, upon which a miniature kneeling Aphrodite is surrounded by four small Cupids. Hellenistic, 3rd century B.C.

4. Earrings with pearls, inlaid stones, and small hanging Cupids wearing the attire of the Oriental god Attis. 1st century B.C.

5. a. Funerary band from the island of Kos, decorated with a procession of sphinxes interspersed with finely wrought rosettes. Archaic Daedalic work of admirable precision in its elaborate Orientalizing ornamentation. Mid-7th century B.C. b. Diadem featuring the 'knot of Herakles' with garnets and some enamel. From the 'Thessalian Treasure', 3rd century B.C.

6. a. Earrings with rosette and a hanging basket, in which a Muse, seated on a bed of foliage, is playing the lyre. Hellenistic, 4th or 3rd century B.C. b. Necklace in the form of a plaited band and small hanging amphorae in three rows; at each end, on a background of green enamel, the granulated inscription: ΖΩΙΛΑC. From the 'Thessalian Treasure', 3rd century B.C.

2

4

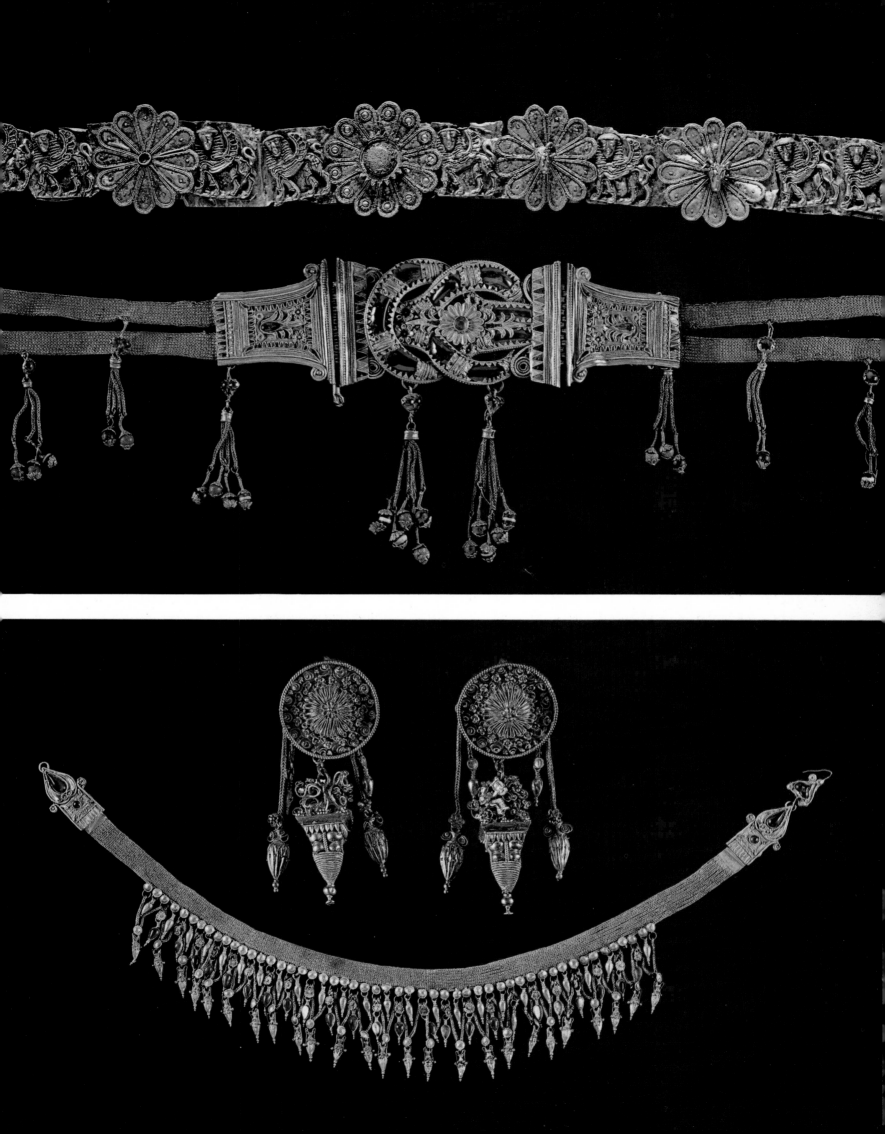

7

a

b

8

c

d

7. a. Crescent-shaped earring with open work design: a monogram between two confronted peacocks; beads and small pearls. 6th-7th century A.D. b. Wide bracelet with disk of open work decoration and circular design with the 'horn of Amaltheia' (the horn of abundance) theme. Probably Syrian, 6th century A.D. c. Pair of crescent-shaped earrings with open work design: a disk with two confronted birds in a nest between two palmettes. 6th-7th century A.D. d. Ring with an enamelled representation of Christ Pantocrator in a square setting and the four beasts of the Apocalypse in small projecting disks. 12th or 13th century.

8. Belt buckle with inlaid stones in the Persian style and with the pomegranate, symbol of fertility and abundance as its motif. Greek work from Constantinople, 18th century A.D.

9. Pendant of rock crystal with Christ Pantocrator in relief. 12th or 13th century. The setting in gold and precious stones is of the 18th century.

10. Pendant in the shape of a one-masted caravel with enamel and hanging pearls. Spanish style, 16th century.

11. Bifacial pendant belonging to Metropolitan Parthenios of Caesarea, with sapphires and emeralds on the one side, and miniature painted enamel disks and inscriptions on the other. Greek specimen from Constantinople, 1738.

9

10

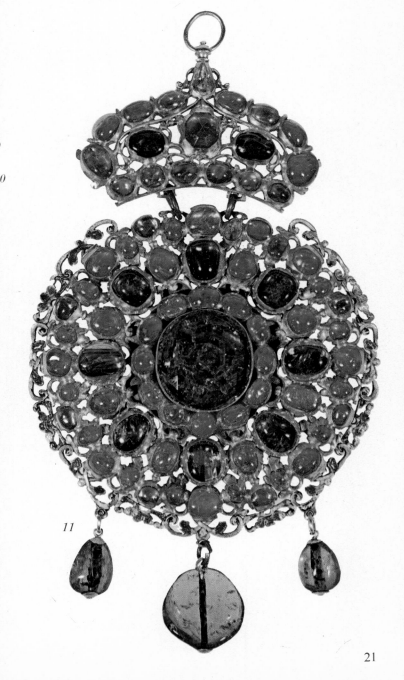

11

21

12. *Fayyum portrait of a young man*. The portraits, which, for religious reasons, were buried with mummies in Egypt, make up the richest surviving collection of portraits of late antiquity. There are about 800 of them. The dark young man of this portrait, painted on linen in 'encaustic' technique, is one of the finest specimens of its kind. *Mid-3rd century A.D.*

13. *Fayyum portrait of a young woman*. The flattened picture and the rather abstracted expression are well-suited to the frontal position and the formal apotropaic gesture. In her left hand the woman is holding the Egyptian cross, the 'ankh'. Female martyrs in Byzantine and post-Byzantine icons are shown in exactly the same posture.

13

14

15

14. *Representation of a female head—possibly the personification of one of the four seasons—clearly influenced by the painting of the Fayyum portraits, on a 'Coptic' woollen fabric. 5th or 6th century A.D.*

15. *'Coptic' fabric from Egypt, with the Pegasus theme in the Persian-Sassanid manner under evident Greek influence. 5th or 6th century A.D.*

16. *Gold-embroidered fabric, the 'aer' used for covering the chalice and paten in the Eucharist, with a symbolic representation of the communion of the Apostles: Christ, under a baldachin, is shown holding a chalice; on his left and right, two Cherubim; a liturgical inscription on the border. 14th century.*

16

17. *Left: Small ivory plaque with representation in relief of St. George, standing. 10th century. Top, right: Bifacial comb made of bone: on one side, a female figure, seated on a throne with ciborium, is holding an orb and a spear; on the other side, a similar figure, less well preserved, is holding a horn of abundance and a palm-frond; she wears a 'polos' on her head. This type of figure was used for the personification of cities; the technique is of the imperial tradition. 5th or 6th century A.D. Bottom, right: Small steatite plaque, representing the Annunciation under a double arch. In the upper section, fragment of a figure; traces of gold and various colours. 12th-13th century.*

18. *Small steatite plaque with a peacefully symmetrical representation of the Presentation at the Temple; incised draperies worn by the tall figures. Last quarter of the 12th century.*

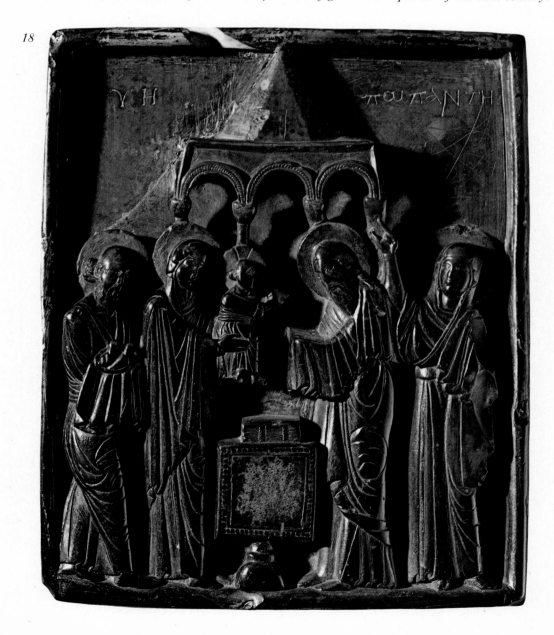

18

19-20. *Two pages from a Psalter. One page pictures Jonah's Ode:
the Prophet, attended by a personification of the Deep, is shown
emerging from the whale and praying in an idyllic landscape; in
the background, a half-hidden villa amidst the delicately graded
shades of the mountains. In contrast to this classicizing representation, the picture of the Three Children in the Fiery Furnace on the
reverse is paratactically arranged in two dimensions. 11th century.*

21. *Gospel with silver cover from Saranda Ekklisies in Thrace.
Gilt filigree decoration with characteristic enamels from that
region. Crucifixion, Resurrection, the Twelve Feasts and the
four beasts of the Apocalypse. Late 18th century.*

19

20

22

23

24

22. *Triptych with the Virgin Mary the 'Portaetissa' from the Iviron Monastery, Saint Paul from the Xeropotamos Monastery and Saint Eleutherios. The blood on Mary's cheek refers to a miracle when the icon was struck by a Saracen on Mount Athos. 15th century.*

23. *The Hospitality of Abraham on an icon of the Palaeologan period: the gentle grace of the angelic figures and the luminous colours alternating with a few darker shades add a poetic touch to this symbolic scene. Late 14th century.*

24. *Saint Demetrios, full-size, holding a lance and shield. The cross was added at a later date. The tall, slender figure of the young warrior, painted around 1500, is in the tradition of the thin, elongated warrior saints of the 14th-15th century.*

25. *The Adoration of the Magi. This is a work in the Venetian style, with the usual motif of ruins, the Magi and their retinue on horseback. The signature: ΧΕΙΡ ΔΟΜΗΝΙΚΟΥ (by the hand of Domenikos) may well belong to the famous Cretan painter Domenico Theotocopuli, better known as El Greco (1541 - 1614), who was still living in Crete in the year 1565. Many Cretan painters painted in both the Byzantine and the Italian styles at that time.*

26. *This complex icon by the Cretan painter Theodore Poulakis comprises scenes from the Genesis, the life of the Virgin Mary, the Dodecaorton (Twelve Feasts), the Second Judgement, etc., arranged in concentric circles. The signature reads: 'Being the result of the labour and art of Theodore Poulakis from Kydonia in the celebrated island of Crete'. 17th century.*

25

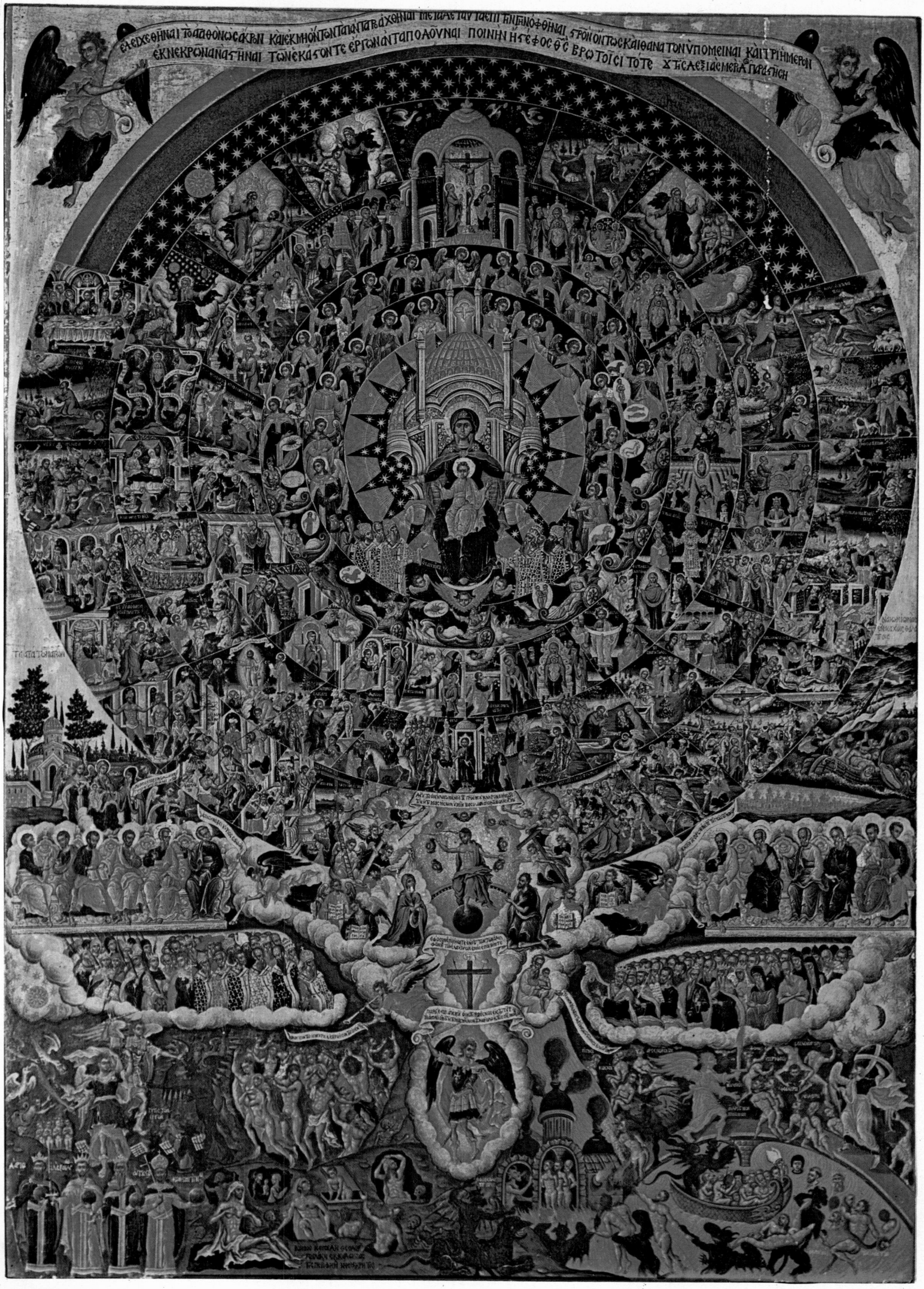

27. *Incense-boat of gold-plated silver and enamel in the shape of a small domed chapel. From the Monastery of St. John the Baptist at Serres, 1613.*

28. *Censer with handle, with embossed representations on the handle and architectural elements on the domed lid. From the collection of relics from Asia Minor, 18th century.*

29. *Pastoral staff with rubies and enamel from Constantinople, belonging to Metropolitan Parthenios of Caesarea. From the collection of relics from Asia Minor, 1738.*

30. *Silver mitre with gilt representations of an Invocation and various saints, probably dating from the 17th century, but restored in 1791. From Argyroupolis, the see of Chaldia in the Pontos.*

31. *Silver litany flabellum with gilt representations and an open work background. From the relics of Asia Minor, 1690.*

32. *19th century cross, from the collection of relics from Asia Minor.*

29

30

31

32

33. *Plate from Nicaea in Asia Minor, with a three-mast schooner, all sails unfurled, and designs on the border copied from Chinese plates. 16th or 17th century.*

34. *Plate, of the kind made for use in churches, decorated with a lion and Oriental flowers. The Greek inscription on the border reads: 'Sun of justice, Christ of our thoughts, our God. 25th May 1666'.*

35-36. *Ceramic eggs from a church chandelier, picturing a two-headed eagle and Seraphim. From Kütahya in Asia Minor, 18th century.*

37. *Jug with painted confronted he-goats and Oriental flowers. Asia Minor pottery from Nicaea, 16th century.*

38. *Flask with painted ships. Asia Minor pottery from Nicaea, 16th century.*

33

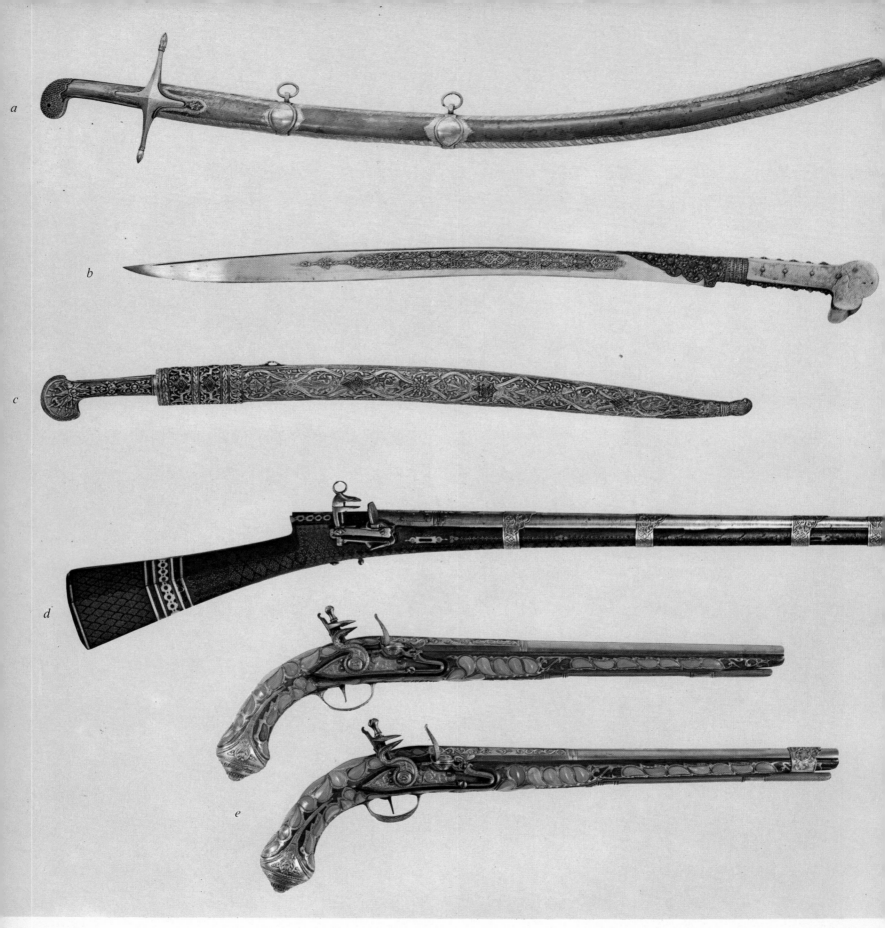

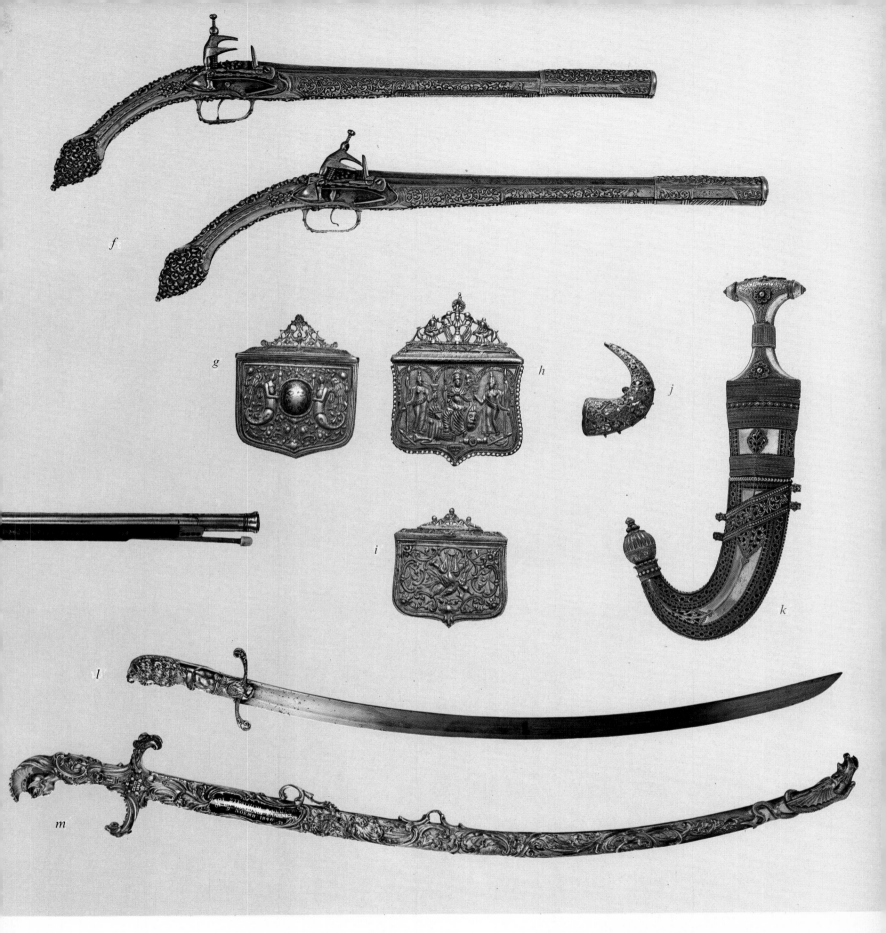

39 a-m. Gun, swords, pistols, and cartridge-cases from the Greek War of Independence and the reign of King Otto. (Several of the arms belonging to the fighters of the War of Independence were spoils of war). a. Sword belonging to Nikolas Petimezas. b. Yataghan belonging to Admiral Yakoumis Tombazis. c. Yataghan with decorated silver scabbard, belonging to the Suliot Photis Tzavellas. d. Muzzle-loader belonging to Nikolas Petimezas; the butt-end is decorated with inlaid mother-of-pearls. e. Pair of pistols decorated with coral. f. Pair of pistols, with embossed silver ornamentation, belonging to Petrobey Mavromichalis. g. Cartridge-case with embossed Gorgon motif, 19th c. h. Cartridge-case, with a representation of Athena between two personifications, belonging to Petrobey Mavromichalis. i. Cartridge-case with embossed decoration. j. Oriental gunpowder-case. k. Dagger with curved blade. l. Sword belonging to General Demetrios Kallergis, with a lion's head in the Classical style decorating the hilt. m. Sword offered to General Demetrios Kallergis by the Greeks of London in 1846 in appreciation of his part in the revolution of 3rd September, 1843.

40

42

43

44

45

42

46

40. *Bedspread from Skyros picturing a horseman who wears 'Frankish' clothes and holds two swords. On the bottom part, a pot of flowers forming a border. 18th-19th century.*

41. *Cushion from Crete. The motif of a Gorgon holding her forked tail dates from ancient Greece, whereas the two-headed eagle is Byzantine. 18th-19th century.*

42. *Nuptial cushion-cover from Jannina: in the centre, the bride and her parents; on the left and right of the group, the bridegroom is shown arriving on horseback; costumes in the Moldovlachian fashion; Oriental flowers in the background, 18th century.*

43. *Cushion from Skyros: a three-mast war schooner embroidered in silk: birds, small human figures, and other motifs in the background. 18th-19th century.*

44. *Detail from a Skyros bedspread: woodcocks in a row within a fanciful setting created by the juxtaposition of flowers and animals in the decoration. 18th-19th century.*

45. *Embroidered border from a Cretan bedspread: two-headed eagles among pots of flowers and other birds. The decoration reflects Western influences. 18th-19th century.*

46. *Sleeveless overcoat from Epeiros with gold embroidery on red felt. 19th century.*

47. *Top: Belt buckle from Epeiros in gold-plated silver filigree. 19th c. Bottom: Belt buckle, from Saframpolis in Asia Minor, of gold-plated silver with semi-precious stones and pieces of coral. 19th century.*

48. *Top left: Earrings in the shape of three-mast caravels hanging from bows. The elegant design and the fine workmanship in gold and enamel reflect Western rococo tendencies. From Siphnos, early 18th c. Bottom left: Earrings with bow and filigree pendants decorated with enamel. From an Aegean island. 18th century? Right: Long earrings, meant to frame the face like the Byzantine imperial 'perpendulia'. Filigree technique with mobile pendent elements. From the island of Kos, 18th century.*

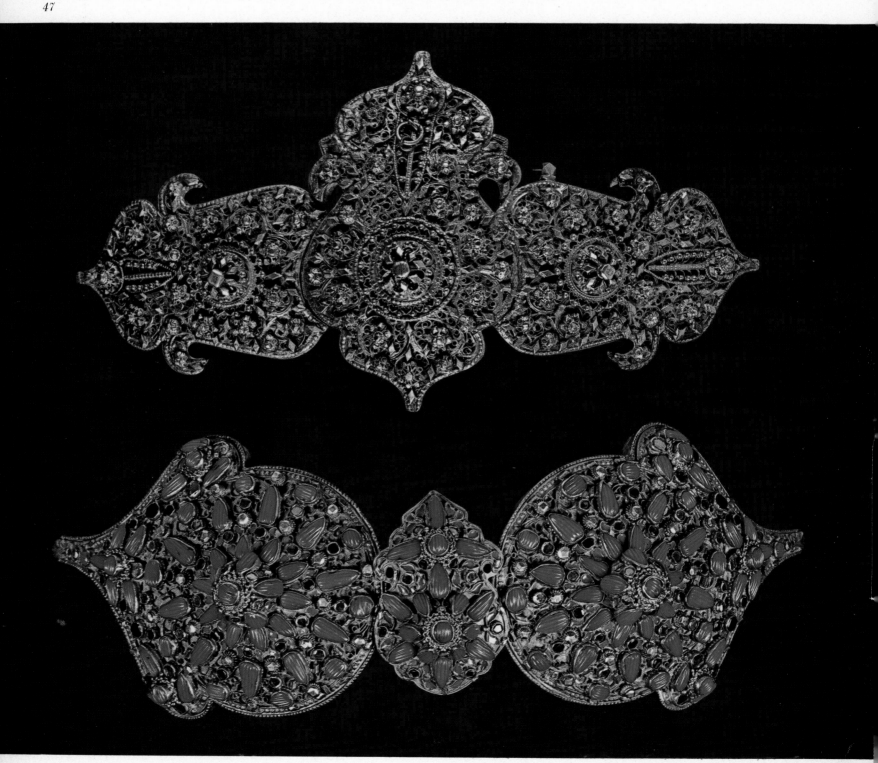

49. *Open work distaff with a representation of Saint George and the inscription: 'Memento 1920'.*

50. *Carved wood-panelling from a reception-room in an upper-class Kozani house, indicative both of the prosperity of that region at the end of the 18th century and of the fine work of Macedonian wood-carvers whose main occupation was the carving of iconostases for churches throughout the Balkans.*

49

50

51. Chest from Skyros, painted in gold and various colours, used for the transportation of bottles containing precious fluids. 18th-19th century.

51

48